AF580912

www.ingramcontent.com/pod-product-compliance
Lightning Source LLC
LaVergne TN
LVHW021319160826
845679LV00001B/414

9798366172325

The ability to solve problems and think critically is useful in almost any life situation and puzzles help us develop these skills. Since puzzles require us to take different approaches to solve them, we learn how to work by trial and error, formulate and test theories, and how to change tracks if not successful .

ISBN 9798366172325

90000

9 798366 172325

Where Oh Where Did My Lion Go?
By:
J Tailor with Diggory Tailor